Introduction

Spiritual Oatmeal and Holy Grits for the soul is a collection of seven devotionals that were written under the inspiration of the Holy Spirit. I am Brightfame a.k.a Bobby with a 'y'. I scribe under the direction of my LORD by the leading of the Spirit of God. I have been called "God's Spiritual Artificial Intelligence". I am honored to walk with HIM so others can see and hear his words through me. This collection of testimonies was written by divine inspiration from God to minister to the body of Christ through the testimony of others. I invite you to sit down and eat this hearty meal. Whether your preference is grits or oatmeal you shall be filled!

Foreword

Spiritual Oatmeal and Holy Grits for the Soul is a collection of testimonies that I have heard from people around the world. The title to this devotional is divinely inspired from an encounter that I had with the Holy Spirit. Oftentimes, my divine inspiration comes while I am running and in fellowship with God. Oatmeal sticks to the bones and grits are a southern morning staple that soothes the belly.

One day I was thinking about how several of my confidants had been asking me to minister to hurting women. I had not shared my personal life stories or testified to them about my past relationships. I am a very private person so I knew that their request came from the LORD. I had decided to leave public ministry shortly after the demise of my late father, Pastor Earlon Bell of Deliverance Church of God In Christ.

However, there became a pull on me to return to the field of ministry after a series of negative events devastated me and painfully impacted my life.

The call to return to ministry was directly mandated to me by the late Sister Sally Mae Pirtle. Sister Sally was a dedicated Woman of God that had attended my late parents' church. This powerful and dedicated Woman of God reconnected with me in the summer of 2023. We had not spoken in years and one day I felt led to call her.

Sister Sally is the neighborhood candy lady, everyone's Big Momma, the spirit filled lady that is everyone's auntie. We picked up where we left off and had a great time talking about the LORD. Unexpectedly, Sister Sally asked me to come and speak to her Bible Study Group in a nearby town. I declined and respectfully explained to her that I love God but I did not preach anymore.

Sister Sally knew me after the Spirit and she persisted three times to invite me to come and preach the gospel like I "used to at our former church". I met her three requests with three denials. Then I agreed to support her in person by listening to her preach and donating to her ministry.

The complete story about the conversation with her is in my book that is soon to be released, *Beauty from Ashes: accept that you are beautifully human and perfectly flawed.* I did not get the opportunity to keep my word to her. Unfortunately, she died shortly after our conversation.

Only then did I realize that I was Peter telling Jesus that I loved Him but I refused to feed HIS sheep. The LORD had used this messenger to summon me to return to ministry. How can I say that I love God if I do not care to lead people to HIM or feed them the word of God? I wept.

There was a strong desire in me to serve God and help people but I did not feel worthy to be used by HIM. I was focused on all of the wrong that I had done and all of the years that I had wasted. God can and will restore all of the wasted years for HIS glory. The LORD reminded me that the gifts and calling that HE places upon our lives are irrevocable. God will never change HIS mind about us and them that He foreknew He called.

Furthermore, I am in good company in the field of evangelism because everyone that He chose to serve HIM were sinners just like me in the Bible. I am in covenant with God so I invite you to partner with us!

My prayer is for you to be strong and courageous! Take a leap of faith and make the decision to repent of your sins and serve the LORD with gladness. Join a church that operates in the five fold ministry and rightly divides the word of God.

The LORD's desire is for you to become rooted and grounded in your faith in Him. I dedicate this devotional to my dear sweet Papa God "And he shall reign over the house of Jacob forever; and of his kingdom there shall be no end (Luke 1:33)".

As always, I most sincerely remain Brightfame a.k.a. Bobby w/ a 'y'.

Tell my story...This has become a recurrent theme in the many conversations that I have had with women. They plead with me to "please feel free to use me as an example when it comes to other people that are hurting and have experienced hardship." People around the world all have something in common, they want to feel secure and loved in a relationship.

I have been fortunate to have some amazing people open up their hearts and share their testimony with me. When they learn that I am a writer then they urge me to share their story with others for encouragement and support. Writing has become therapeutic for me because it allows me to release that which is within me.

Journaling is one of the many spiritual disciplines that strengthens the believer. Creating a log of the past allows one to reflect upon their life and see their failures as and growth over the years. Your past is a reminder to keep moving forward and that you survived the challenges that sought to take you out.

My goal is to remain true to the stories that I have been told by these victorious women. I want to share their faith walk with others to provide them encouragement and support in their time of desperate need.

I am honored to share the testimony of others through written epistles to honor God and defeat the evil one. I encourage you to keep a diary or journal to record the events of your life. The hardest part about writing is to just start. Take the time to read your entries and reflect upon your past and analyze your growth and progress.

My prayer is that you are blessed by the entries within this devotional and your life is positively impacted. Revisit this book and read it as many times as you need to and read the scriptures associated with each testimony. I pray that you will receive a new revelation from the LORD every time. Please share this devotional with others to enrich and enhance their lives.

Volume 1
The Book of Eunice
II Timothy 1:2-5 KJV

Eunice is a native of Ghana and I was privileged to meet this beautiful woman of God through her husband Pastor Emmanuel. There were a series of supernatural events that were orchestrated by the handiwork of God that led to this sisterhood. After engaging in prayer every morning for the fourth watch for several weeks I was introduced to this spiritual giant.

The voice on the other end of the phone had a beautiful and soft sweet accent. There was a strength and femininity that was apparent in her conversation that drew me towards her. Eunice is humble and bold in all things concerning our LORD.

She lovingly teased me about the connection that I had with her husband. The two of them are approximately twenty years my junior but she stated that "she knew that God was in the midst of our spiritual relationship". Otherwise she would be fighting with a woman that drew the attention of her spouse. This discerning woman of God knew her husband after the flesh and Spirit and she had not seen him take such a strong spiritual interest in other people.

She shared that he was constantly praying for me and my family and that he loved me as a family member. She felt compelled to join in his daily prayer routine and lift my family up in prayer.

Eunice shared with me that she was pursuing her nursing degree and this connected us even more. I have been a Registered Nurse for twenty five years and I am a practicing Advance Practice Registered Nurse.

Our fellowship included discussing our family, faith and healthcare practice. I was elated to hear about how she advocated for her patient's and selflessly dedicated herself and resources in order to meet their needs. She had a dream of coming to the United States to grow in her practice and explore new opportunities.

I listened to her speak about her family life and how she and her spouse supported each other as one unit. While she was doing her clinical assignments her spouse would take care of their children at home.

Their youngest child was a toddler at the time so he required complete care and monitoring. The two of them provided consistent continuity of care within their home and nothing went lacking when either of them were away. For example, her husband engaged in countless hours of evangelism which required him to be away from home.

This woman of God completed her obligation regarding evangelism in the surrounding communities by supporting her husband during his absence from their home.

While he was away his mind was clear to minister to the hopeless and dying because everything at home was in order under Eunice. Upon his return he could simply pick up where he had left off with his local ministry. Shalom, nothing was missing and nothing was broken.

One day Eunice told me that she wanted to share her personal testimony with me about her past. Respectfully, she discussed it with the High Priest of her household and they decided that it was of the LORD.

Pastor and I had been praying for the LORD's will regarding reconciliation with my past mate once he was reconciled to the LORD.

After Eunice became aware of our dedicated morning prayers she wanted to share her life story with me. Eunice told me that the LORD had spoken to her concerning me. The LORD had told her that "Bobby is a counselor". My past experiences were not in vain and the LORD was restoring my many wasted years for HIS glory.

Then she wanted me to remember the story of the prodigal son. The father missed his son that had fallen and he longed for reconciliation. However, the son had free will and had chosen to live according to his own fleshly desires.

The son hit rock bottom and he came to himself and repented of his sins. Then his right mind returned to him and he desired to reconcile with his father that he had wronged.

Eunice stated that the father only had to be open to reconcile to his son after his son had been reconciled back to God. The father did not look for his son, he did not offer his son bribes or beg him to return to his rightful place and position in HIS kingdom. People that are out of God's perfect will and position will not prosper or have total peace that surrendering to his LORDSHIP of Jesus Christ brings.

Eunice testified that she had been in love in the past with another man before she married Emmanuel. This man is the father of her middle child and she desired for their family to stay together. Ultimately, she wanted this man to surrender to the will of God, marry her and be a loving father to their children. This is a noble desire for a woman to have and it is within the perfect will of God.

Marriage is honorable and the Lord blesses a man with a godly wife that brings him favor. Her desire was far from the stark reality of her relationship with the man. The man devalued her and his child for many years.

Her life was riddled with pain and disappointment as he took her for granted and refused to be the man that God created HIM to be. Prayer became her portion and her tears were her meat for many years.

The pain from his rejection became unbearable and the enemy began to torment her mind with thoughts of suicide and homicide. A voice would tell her to place her child in the refrigerator because she would be better off in heaven.

Then she would personally experience torment from thoughts in her mind that told her to end her pain by taking her own life. Since this man did not want her or her children then she must not be worthy of love. The devil taunted her with thoughts of worthlessness and tried to convince her that she did not matter and that she would not be missed.

As a medical professional she witnesses others that struggle with their mental health. She added that without God in their life there is no opposing voice to challenge those imaginations within them because they do not serve Him.

Ultimately, she fought those demonic imaginations and tormenting thoughts through the word of God and prayer. On the appointed day her deliverance came and the LORD directed her towards a friend that could assist her with spiritual healing and restoration.

Pastor Emmanuel had been her best friend for over six years. Through a spiritual relationship with God they battled her infirmities and struggles together. God let Eunice know that it was time for her to move on because he had rejected the man that she had wanted to marry. Furthermore, the Holy Spirit reminded her that she had written down the characteristics that she desired to have in a spouse in her diary dated 2011.

The man was disqualified from being her spouse and from leading her children in the direction of the Kingdom of God. The man had chosen idolatry, he was serving himself and he was embracing carnality. They were going in two separate directions and two cannot walk together unless they are in agreement.

Eunice lifted herself up, raised up from her prayer position on the floor and accepted the final decision of her LORD. The imaginations within her head disappeared and the destructive spirit fled from her. Once she was healed then she actually began to see Pastor Emmanuel as the LORD saw him. This man of God was a man that saw her as a wife. This godly man was future driven and he had vision.

Furthermore, he loved another man's children as if they were his own. This man was worthy of her because he had surrendered to the will of God and he would walk with her as the high priest of their household. Later the pair married and moved into a comfortable place with their children.

Their marriage has been reflective of a healthy spiritual union that is God centered. The entire family is thriving and doing the work of the LORD in their community.

Eunice's former mate found her on a social media site and asked her to reconcile. She let him know that it was too late, she was happily married and faithfully serving God. The man was persistent in his attempt to win her back with his words. Eunice remained steadfast in her faith in God and refused to allow herself to be seduced by the enemy.

The LORD had spoken and it was not within HIS perfect will for her to have a relationship with this man. There are other variables that she weighed in order to determine whether or not it was healthy for the children to be trusted with him.

Nonetheless, everyone was healthy and thriving in their present living arrangement so altering their routine to accommodate him was not an option.

The book of Eunice is a living Epistle that I am honored to write on behalf of this amazing Woman of God. Eunice is reflective of Timothy's mother because she served the LORD and left a spiritual inheritance for her lineage.

I count it a blessing that the LORD allowed me to meet Eunice and be privileged to share her testimony. She is a courageous and ambitious warrior within the Kingdom of God that has the ability of a sniper.

Although she comes across as timid and is soft spoken, the anointing that rests upon her life is without measure and it is sure to set the captive free. Our goal in this ministry is to expose the tactics and schemes of Satan so people can recognize him in their situation.

We want to advance the Kingdom of God through the ministry of deliverance to annihilate the works of the enemy upon your life for good.

This concludes the First volume of the Book of Eunice.

Volume 2
The Book of Emmanuel
The second Book of Eunice
Matthew 1:23b

Once I completed the first book of Eunice I called her to clarify a few points. She asked me to hold on for a moment while she asked her Papa, Pastor Emmanuel for permission to speak to me freely about her past. Emmanuel agreed, she politely excused herself from his presence then she took a deep breath and exhaled very slowly.

I could feel the tension in the air and I prepared myself for what I perceived would be an emotional encounter. Eunice gathered herself and softly stated that she has to mentally prepare herself to share her entire testimony with me.

There were a vast array of emotions that she had dealt with and continued to battle with due to circumstances that were beyond her control. Although she had mastered the imaginations that tormented her inside of her head she still wrestled with social stigma within the Ghanan culture because of her past.

Eunice needed another chapter within this faith filled devotional because her testimony has to be heard around the world. I would be the bold voice for her and other women that have been silenced due to cultural bias.

This woman is a fierce lioness like myself but she had to exercise restraint and remain silent due to the region that she lived in. She reasoned that people judged her for being a single mother of two beautiful children even though they did not know her story. The pain in her voice during this interview was palpable.

I knew that she needed an outlet to alleviate her distress. She spoke while I listened intently and took notes. Eunice deserved another chapter to tell her story to the world because one volume would not give her or her family the justice that they deserve.

I find it fitting to name this book after our LORD and Savior Emmanuel and her husband because these are the two men that she credits with rescuing her from destruction of the enemy. I am proud to present the second volume of the Book of Eunice.

The Book of Emmanuel is dedicated to Eunice in honor of our LORD and Savior Jesus Christ and her Papa, Pastor Emmanuel Hortovi, the prayer warrior that intercedes for countless hours on end.

Eunice began this session by answering my question about the fathers of her two elder children. She explained that all of her children have different fathers and she had experienced judgment by the locals because of it.

She started by telling me that she loved all of her children and that they are a blessing from God. Emmanuel loved all of their children equally and their children loved him as their father. Their eldest child is a girl and she is the apple of Emmanuel's eye and he has claimed her as his own child since her birth.

Eunice was a young and ambitious healthcare student that was studying abroad with a female confidant. They attended school and went to clinical in order to obtain their nursing license. During their downtime they desired to get out and mingle as single young women. Since they were in an unfamiliar territory they thought that it was best to ask a trustworthy gentleman to escort them around town.

While they were at the hospital completing their required clinical hours they had met an administrator that took a special interest in Eunice. She described the gentleman as a short middle aged, overweight dark skinned male.

Clearly, a relationship with him would be a conflict of interest and considered fraternizing. Besides, she was not attracted to him and she was focused on her studies. The night that they decided to hit the town they agreed to call him for a ride.

The astute young ladies agreed to go out together and they felt like his esteemed position would make him accountable. They reached out to him and he agreed to pick them up and show them the area.

Once he arrived Eunice's roommate declined the invitation and stated that she would stay at home. Eunice was a polite and respectful young lady and because she had initiated the call with him she felt obligated to go out. Furthermore, she did not want to question her roommate in front of the hospital administrator.

The gentleman told her that his uncle was running for a political office and they could go to his campaign party. Eunice was slightly uncomfortable but she reasoned within herself that there would be other professionals there.

Upon arrival she decided to remain in the car and she told him that she would wait for him to leave. Shortly after he entered the residence he returned to his car to find her sleeping. They departed and he took a different route to take her home. She inquired about the route and he told her that he had to drop off some paperwork for the campaign.

They arrived at another house and he invited her inside. Again she politely declined but he urged her to come inside for her own safety. She stepped out of the car and told him that she would take her chances outside and allow him to go inside alone. Suddenly, his temperment changed and he became physically aggressive with her and they began to fight.

Although she was no physical match for this man she fought him with all of her might. After what seemed like several hours she became exhausted and succumbed to his abuse. Overpowered by him, she was taken inside of the residence against her will and sexually assaulted.

The man took her home and she never had further interactions with him. She was traumatized, ashamed and terrified of what could happen to her if she reported him to the authorities. She went through the various stages of grief and blamed herself and her roommate for the tragic event. Her faith in God sustained her throughout this time but she struggled with forgiveness.

Eunice was an aspiring health professional with many male suitors that took a special interest in her. Now she suffered from trust issues and was experiencing low self esteem. One of the men that she had become fond of was a physician that worked at the facility she did clinical at.

She trusted this clinician and decided to share with him the tragic events that had taken place with the administrator. The physician was empathetic and he told her that he seriously considered marrying her one day.

She had been feeling unwell and she thought that she was developing malaria. Eunice sought medical attention and learned that she was pregnant. She shared this with her roommate who advised that if she had known about the episode sooner she would have offered her contraception.

Eunice was naive and did not understand the concept of contraception at the time. She decided to tell the doctor that she was with child and she was disappointed at his response. The physician advised her to abort the fetus because he did not want to raise another man's child. Eunice stated that this went against her faith in God and she refused to have the procedure. The physician cut off all communication with her and eventually transferred to another hospital.

Eunice told her brother about the sexual assault and he challenged her accusation by asking her if she was sure that the administrator had raped her. Then she told Emmanuel, a friend of her brother that she knew from church and he supported her decision to keep her daughter.

Emmanuel began to claim the newborn as his own and he provided financial and spiritual support for her as well. They became the best of friends and he would routinely check on her to make sure that she was remaining steadfast in her faith in God. Eunice knew that Emmanuel was attracted to her but she only saw him as a friend.

Eunice decided to move on and began dating; she was a single mother now and she had to choose a good father for her child. She and a fellow nurse became attracted to each other and they began to date. This man could provide financial security and worked in a noble profession. He began to speak about the desire to marry her early on but she noticed that he was lacking in intimacy.

The relationship worked but it felt more like an arrangement. She had moved in with him and had taken on the role of a dutiful wife but was not receiving the benefits of a spouse. She would rise up early in the morning and complete chores and then she would cook him three meals a day.

There were a list of clear expectations but there was never any sincere affection or praise. The sacrifices that she made regarding long hours of travel to appease this man went unnoticed.

Eventually, she became the recipient of persistent negative feedback and harsh criticism. This man had created a list of the attributes that he wanted in a wife and at the top of his list was vanity.

Eunice was subjected to his cruelty when he would blatantly criticize her to his ex girlfriends on the phone and compare her to them. During their three year relationship she became pregnant and gave birth to a son. Now she had to think about the future of her two children so she decided to turn to the LORD for direction.

Eunice believed in the power of prayer so she began to seek God for this man to give his life to the LORD. She fasted and prayed without ceasing and she was determined to marry him. There was no change in this man and she had to beg him to even tell her that he loved.

Occasionally, he obliged her and confessed his adoration but when he spoke she knew that it was not heart felt. Finally, she realized that this was not the man of God that she desired to marry and build a family with. Eunice left him and ventured out on her own as a single mother of two and decided to raise her children to serve the LORD.

Eunice would see Emmanuel at church and he would give her financial assistance to her even when it left him penniless. Emmanuel told her that he had always loved her as a wife and that he felt responsible for her failed relationships because he never asked her to date.

Eunice shared with me that she only saw him as a friend so he could not rescue her from her past. Time passed and she would only encounter Emmanuel on occasion but one day when she saw him she noticed him. She states that he was a good height and had a nice haircut.

Amazingly, she was attracted to him and she agreed to date him. Their courtship went extremely well but Eunice was still struggling with her past trauma so she lacked trust in men. Oftentimes, she would find herself trying Emmanuel to see if he was sincere.

Emmanuel genuinely walked out his faith in God and he was so unselfish that she was in disbelief. There were times that she knew that he was down to his last two dollars and he would give it to her even though she had money on hand. Somehow when this man gave his last he ended up having his needs supernaturally met.

She witnessed the power of God in his life and she was drawn to God even more through him. Emmanuel proposed and although she was a little hesitant to commit she agreed to marry him. People judged her for being a single mother with children from two different men. They made her feel unworthy of being engaged to a man of the cloth.

Eunice served the LORD and she knew the truth about her past so she fought for her happiness with Emmanuel. They set the wedding day and as the day drew near she developed cold feet. When she shared her doubt about their future with her fiancee' he would simply tell her not to worry that he was praying for her.

On their wedding day the church was filled with family and friends. When she walked down the aisle to become Mrs. Emmanuel Hotorvi she watched her future husband praise the LORD. Pastor Emmanuel was focused on the LORD and his future wife, he was caught up in praise and worship during their nuptials. Her family labeled him as the preacher that speaks in other tongues.

Their marriage has been God's design and she never imagined that a man could love her this way. She told me that she would not have believed a prophet if they told her that she would marry a man of God and that he would love her unconditionally.

Miraculously, the Holy Spirit reminded her of the diary dated 2011. Eunice wrote an entry that stated that she wanted to marry a man that would love God and love her unconditionally.

The LORD heard her request and He orchestrated this marital union in order to demonstrate HIS love to her. God desires to see us equally yoked together with another believer. Two is better than one for if one falls the other can lift them up (Ecc 4:9-10). God desires to bring healing and restoration to us and our families.

This completes the Book of Emmanuel,
The Second Volume of The Book of Eunice.

Volume 3
The Book of Rebecca
I Samuel 1:27

There was a fleet of police cars arriving at the campus so I inquired about the situation. I was on duty as a Registered Nurse so I thought that it was prudent to evaluate the encounter for safety. I was reassured that there was no real threat and that everything was under control.

I surveyed the scene, read the police report and patient profile and agreed with the supervisor. Once I laid eyes upon the patient I had a reassurance from the LORD that there would be no violent outburst. There was a documented history of oppositional defiance but we would not witness a temper tantrum today.

God is and always stays in control but today was different, he had plans for this gentleman that involved HIM. I left the building and began to pray and ask God what he wanted me to do. Shortly afterwards I was led to meet the parent of this client.

I received prophetic words that this young man was adopted by a single woman. He was also the victim of substance abuse while in utero, his appearance was consistent with fetal alcohol syndrome but there was also drug and sexual addiction through his mother.

The father was absent and his mother likely did not know who the father was due to her bondage to addiction. Nonetheless, the LORD loved this young man and he desired to love him with an everlasting love and father HIM.

Upon returning to the building I completed a quick assessment on him and asked him who he lived with and he stated that he lived with his mother. I asked him about his father and he replied with "I have never met him and I do not care". I told him that I was sorry that he did not have a relationship with his dad.

Then I noticed a look on his face that was worthy of mention. I could not put words to the expression but it spoke to me and I asked the LORD what I was witnessing. I heard a word in my head that I have never used before so I looked it up to see what it meant. The Holy Spirit spoke "chagrin" and when I looked it up it described the look on his face that exposed what emotion that he was feeling at the moment.

Oxford dictionary defines it as distress and or embarrassment at having failed or being humiliated. This word accurately described the condition of this young man and I knew that he was tormented by this emotional state.

I heard that his mother had arrived so I volunteered to greet her and walk her to the waiting area. I met this flamboyant, down to earth red head that was 5 feet tall and well built. This friendly outspoken middle aged mother lugged her large purse on her shoulder, and walked through the security entrance while asking for a morning snack and some water to take her medications. She added that she had PTSD, hypertension, anxiety, bipolar disorder and a whole host of other diagnoses.

Immediately, I liked her demeanor and her transparency about her need for help with both situations. I introduced myself and told her that I would escort her to the patient. I was overwhelmed with the pertinent information from her during our stroll to the unit. She told me who his psychiatrist was, how long she expected her son to be admitted and all about his present behaviors.

The staff were not ready for Rebecca so I sat down with her and allowed her to vent. She told me that she has had him since he was a few days old. Recently, he had run away from home and she was unable to locate him. This morning he decided that he wanted to come back home and she was elated.

She shared that she had a hard time getting him to obey the rules and keeping him calm. He was born addicted to drugs and alcohol and his mother wanted her to take him until she could get herself through drug and alcohol rehabilitation. Due to the brain damage that he suffered in utero he had violent outbursts, mental health and social challenges and self esteem issues.

She further explained that he struggles in school and that lately he had worked himself up because he has to take Spanish this fall. He was feeling a great deal of distress over having to speak a new language in front of others.

Lately he was ruminating over the embarrassment that he would endure over failing in front of his peers. Chagrin had been his portion throughout his life and his struggle was not even his fault.

The patient had been off of his prescribed medications so his emotions were out of control. I noticed scratches on his face and arm and different bruises that were at various stages of healing to the side of Rebecca's face. There had been physical altercations between the two of them that required her to restrain him for both of their safety.

Rebecca cried as she told me how she had fought for resources for her son. This woman spent countless hours praying for him, taking him to a Bible teaching church and signing him up for male mentors. Many of the mentors became overwhelmed with the rituals that he went through to calm himself and they abandoned their assignment.

The church attendance helped but he needed more structure on a consistent basis then a weekly youth service brings. She volunteered with the local police department to ensure that her son would have rapport with law enforcement.

Monthly she would serve the local police department on National Holidays and for local events to thank them for protecting her son. He had many encounters with law enforcement as a juvenile and she feared that one day he would be an adult that could be viewed as a menace to society. This mother used wisdom to develop strategies to provide natural and spiritual protection for her son.

I gave him instructions to put on a pair of non-skid socks so he would be less likely to fall. I also instructed him to give his shoes to his mother so she could take them home. She had mentioned that the sneakers were not his and that she had brought a pair of shoes that were acceptable with our protocol. The young man had been institutionalized many times before so she came prepared to leave him for a prolonged period of time for treatment.

He responded to my instructions by removing his shoes and giving them to his mother but he reasoned that he was wearing his own socks. I replied with "the rules state that you have to put on our socks for safety and when you are in my house you must follow the rules".

Immediately, he removed his socks and gave them to his mother and put on the hospital approved socks. His mother cried and said I asked him why he does not follow the rules at home and he told me that the facility provides him with structure and he needs to follow a routine.

The LORD had told me that he would not be a problem and that we would not witness any violent outbursts. I told his mother that there are some things that are non negotiable and children need routine and structure. I am an adult and I expect a child to respond as a child not like a parent or an adult so they do.

They completed the process of getting him evaluated and we continued our conversation about their life. Rebecca shared her faith in God with me and I was all ears. She loved God and her zeal for him was apparent in her mannerisms and excitement about Him.

She attended a weekly Bible study and was part of a prayer group. I listened to her quote scriptures while she lifted her hands and gave thanks to the LORD. Then she told me how lonely she was at one time and that she prayed to God for a man.

Rebecca prayed and told God that she wanted him to send her a man. She wanted a man that she could love and that would love her, she did not care if he was bald or if he had teeth. She told God that she was willing to buy her man some teeth if she had to, she was willing to accept a young or old man, black or white.

God never sent her a husband so she stated that her prayer went unanswered. One day Rebecca received a phone call from Child Protective Services and the agent told her that a woman had named her as a potential foster mother for her newborn. Rebecca confirmed that she knew the woman to the agent. He added that the child was born with fetal alcohol syndrome and addicted to drugs.

Rebecca stated that she was not in a position to take a newborn, especially one that had disabilities. The man told her that he was about to go on vacation and that his wife would kill him if he brought another kid home. He told her that he had three biological children and that he adopted two from his job.

He reasoned with her and asked her if he could just come and see her place. Then he could approve her to take the newborn for two weeks and that if it was not a good fit then he would find foster care. Rebecca told the agent that it was a newborn human being, not a puppy.

This woman of God's heart broke for the infant and she agreed to let the agency evaluate her home. The man gave her his approval and brought the newborn to her. The infant spent several weeks with her and his mother relinquished her parental rights.

Rebecca had fallen in love with him so she adopted him as her son.

Rebecca shared her testimony about how she became a mother with a woman in her Bible Study group and the woman began to laugh. Rebecca did not understand the woman's reaction to her testimony. The lady told her that when you pray to God you have to be more specific.

The woman replied with " you asked God for a man, not a husband." You are the one that said that you would love any man that HE gave you that would love you back. You told Him that you would accept a man that was bald, young and toothless that needed you.

You did not tell God that you did not want a baby. God answered your prayer when He blessed you with your son. Rebecca smiled when she joyfully shared her epiphany with me and told me that she was satisfied with the answer to her prayer.

I Samuel 1:27 states that I prayed for this child and the LORD has granted my request.

This is the Book of Rebecca.

Volume 4
The Book of Jen
Ephesians 6:4

You are a writer? Feel free to use me and tell my story, said Jennifer the In House Supervisor. I had only known Jen for a few years and my opinion of her was that she was strong willed and assertive. This woman had a strong background in Emergency Medicine and she was my type of person.

I had twelve years of experience as an Emergency Advance Practice Registered Nurse.

My Emergency Medicine healthcare providers will know what I am talking about when I say that she spoke the E.R. lingo and they would totally get Jen. When I arrived at work in the morning she would greet me with a hug and state that she was glad that I was on duty.

Jen is the co-worker that tests boundaries and will challenge authority if indicated. Nonetheless, she is the type of nurse that I would want if I could not advocate for myself. After three years of working with her in an acute mental hospital this is all that I knew about her.

Jen was promoted to a campus leadership nursing role so my interactions with her were very limited. We would pass each other while reporting to duty some mornings. She would usually have her sunglasses on top of her head, carry a large cup of coffee and smoke a cigarette before starting her shift.

Jen and I would respond to medical emergencies and work as a two man team to stabilize and transfer patients to a higher level of care. I could see her passion and empathy for others through her dedicated practice. One morning I was working as a Registered Nurse and I needed to leave before shift change.

Jen came in early that morning and she stated that she had a mandatory class to attend. She volunteered to cover my unit until the day shift nurse arrived so I could clock out. I gave her hand off and then she mentioned her children. This discussion about her children led her to talk about her family.

When Jen began to tell me her story I saw a different side of her. I realized that I had only met the nurse Jen. Now I was privileged to meet the Jen who had a broken past. Amazingly, this is wherein lied her strength because in her brokenness she displayed the power of God. In our weakness His strength is made perfect.

While Jen shared her testimony with me I sat there motionless and glued to every word that came out of her mouth. Jen told me that she had two school aged children with her ex husband. She proudly stated that she had a son and a daughter. Their father was a good provider and even though he had trouble with maintaining employment the entrepreneur within him made him resourceful.

Their daughter adored her father and he was a good mentor to their son. He would cut his son's hair and give both of their children love and affection. Unfortunately, this man's affection would extend beyond their family and it would be given to strange women.

Jen added that her ex spouse was a self proclaimed ladies man and that his weakness was sexual sin. Their marriage was a series of infidelity and forgiveness without any real transformation.

They both wanted to remain married and make the marriage work so they decided to join a local church for support. Jen stated that this decision to allow God into their relationship made the world of difference. They enjoyed many years of wedding bliss and they regularly fellowshipped with other families and married couples during the week.

They were dedicated to their local church and they served in any capacity that they could to honor God. She did not grow up in church so this was what she felt like she had been missing out on.

One day she was taking a shower and she heard her spouse sobbing. Jen stated that her husband never cried so she wrapped a towel around her pregnant body and went to console him. When she inquired of him what was wrong he tearfully stated that a neighbor had approached him about a serious matter.

Her husband told her that the neighbor said that the woman that lives across the street was just released from the hospital and she abandoned her newborn baby. The woman added that the postpartum mother told her that the baby belonged to Jen's husband. Her husband admitted that he had been having an affair with the married mother of two.

He denied knowing that she was pregnant which Jen believed because the woman had an addiction to crack cocaine and was thin. Jen got up off of the couch and went across the street to confront the situation . There was a colorful discussion with Jen and the married couple about the abandoned newborn.

The spouse of the mistress did not know that his wife was pregnant or that she had abandoned her newborn. Jen returned home to tell her husband that he needed to do right by this newborn if he was the father.

The newborn was taken in by his maternal uncle until they could establish paternity. The adultress went on to live with her husband and children as usual. Jen's husband and her worked through the ordeal with the help of their church. Jen and her husband attained an attorney and sought to establish paternity through D.N.A. testing.

Over the course of six years they sought to establish paternity while petitioning the court for custody. When the results finally arrived Jen was relieved. Her husband had fathered this child and she stated that they needed to bring their son home.

Jen reasoned with her husband that they lived in a small town so the children may meet each other. What if his son fell in love with his sister? What if their two sons met under negative circumstances and became enemies? She reasoned that they needed to unite their children and raise them up as siblings.

Her husband understood and then he took it upon himself to sign away his paternity rights to his son's maternal uncle without Jen's knowledge. Soon after Jen learned that her husband had rescinded his paternal rights she fell apart. This led to the end of their marriage and their departure from the church that they had grown to love.

Jen explained to me that she viewed this as the ultimate act of betrayal from her spouse. They had agreed to bring their son home and raise him as their own child. How could her husband selfishly make a decision that impacted their entire family without her?

The decision to leave the church stemmed from a belief that they would discourage the dissolution of the marriage. Jen had nothing left within her to fight for the future of her family to stay together. Jen had wrestled with infidelity, betrayal and now she was dealing with a truce breaker. They divorced and she moved on with her life and began to rebuild as a single parent of two children.

One day her son came home with a note stating that he had gotten into a fight at school. She followed up with the school and she was grieved to learn that the other child involved in the kerfuffle was her son's half brother. Jen feared that this would happen and she spiraled into a depression after this incident.

A former church member reached out to her and offered to take her to lunch. The acquaintance added that she was not interested in trying to counsel her about her marital dissolution.

Jen agreed to join her because she missed their fellowship. Jen shared her journey that led to the divorce with her former church mate. This lady knew Jen's personal childhood story and she spoke a word of wisdom into Jen's life.

Jen was the offspring of a teenage mother that had gotten pregnant by a married man that was ten years her senior. Jen was raised by her teenage mother along with her maternal grandmother. As a young child she was told that her father was a married man with children and she even knew who he was.

However, her father never acknowledged that she was his child. Many years passed and she remembers meeting her siblings, visiting his house and her mother speaking to his ex wife.

Nonetheless, she was never officially named as one of his children, her father even refused to sign her birth certificate. Upon his death bed she visited him as he lay sick and dying of terminal cancer; even then he refused to claim her as his daughter.

Jen attended his funeral out of respect for his contribution to her life. Sadly, her name was not listed on the obituary along with his other children. Respectfully, her siblings invited her to sit with the family during the service because they knew the truth. Jen would not receive the closure that she deserved from this man that she knew to be her biological father.

Her sister in Christ told her that the reason that he did not acknowledge that she was his daughter was because he was guilty of a crime. Jen's mother was a fifteen year old child when this twenty five year old married father took advantage of her.

The pregnancy was unplanned and a signature on the birth certificate or the establishment of paternity could have sent him to prison. This man was ashamed of the crime that he had committed and he wanted to save his own skin.

The pain that Jen felt from the betrayal of her ex husband was deeply rooted within the betrayal that she had experienced from her own trauma. Jen cried when she told me this part of her story so I knew that she empathized with her stepson. The mother, nurse and humanitarian was alive and evident in this Woman of God.

Ephesians 6:4 warns the fathers not to provoke their children to become angry but to raise them up in love and to admonish them. Jen's story is a testimony of how the failure of a father to demonstrate the love of God in the life of their children can traumatize them.

Fortunately, for Jen she found love in her maternal family and her Heavenly Father. The blessing of two beautiful children gave her the strength to seek healing for her soul wounds. We serve a just God and He will right every wrong in due season.

The LORD instructed me to correct the obituary of her late father because it was designed with an error. Our Heavenly Father released to me the writer's pen as His scribe to set things in order.

The obituary now reads as follows: John Nelson is survived by his four children, Staci Nelson, Daniel Nelson, Jennnifer Nelson Hamer-Hill and Kevin Nelson. He leaves behind many other family members and a host of friends to grieve him. John Nelson shall forever be remembered as the father of four beautiful children and his genetic connection to each of them shall forever be established in Heaven and on earth! Amen.

Although he failed during his lifetime to acknowledge one very important life that his seed created; we choose to remember and celebrate his life through the legacy of our Beloved Jen!

Many of our lives are filled with regret because of our past decisions. I want to challenge you to find the courage to correct the mistakes that you have made while you still have time. I stand in as a proxy for John Nelson and speak on his behalf.

Jennifer is a daughter that would make any father proud. Obviously, there was greatness within John because the world received the gift of Jen through him.

John Nelson will forever be remembered through the legacy of Jennifer because she is like the wild cactus. A cactus is a unique type of plant or flower that has a pinprick surface. The tough outer layer serves as a protective covering to preserve the life giving force that is nested within it. When one is thirsty and in need of hydration the cactus has the ability to sustain their life.

We honor Jennifer for sharing the gift of the living water through her career and her testimony. Jen, your Heavenly Father loves you unconditionally and your love for him is evident through your service and contributions to others.

This my dear sweet friends is the volume of The Book of our Beloved, cactus flower, Jen.

Volume 5
The Book of Betty Lou
Revelation 1:7

This biography is personal to me
because it is about my late mother, the great
Betty Lou Bell. My mother is best described as
a martyr like the honorable Mother Teresa. My
earliest childhood memories were of her
spending countless hours cooking full course
meals and delivering plates of soul food to
those that were sick and shut in.

My siblings and I would sit nearby the kitchen and salivate over the variety of foods on the kitchen counter. She would forbid us from taking one bite and educate us that servanthood is our reasonable service. We would go with her to deliver the meals to those that were in need.

One gentleman that she would take meals to had a left above the knee amputation. He used a wheelchair for mobility, so when we arrived he would struggle to open the door and accept the meals.

We would enter his home and place the food on the kitchen counter for him. In hindsight I realize that his living conditions were very poor and that his home was not fit for someone disabled to live in. This man was able to remain in his home because of the contributions that were made to him.

My mother was also very active in our local church, East Seventeenth Church of God In Christ. The Pastor was Bishop Hurley Bassett and he routinely traveled from a nearby state to lead the church. My father was ordained as an Elder and he served in the ministry as a preacher and church worker.

My mother would volunteer to clean the church, decorate, prepare meals and chair an annual Pastor's appreciation service. One day I overheard some ladies taking credit for cleaning the church and paying for the church decorations.

I ran to my mother and told her about their false claims. My mother silenced me and told me that everything that she did was conducted in secrecy before our LORD.

I did not understand why she would not take credit for the hard work that she did because she deserved the recognition for her contributions. As a mature believer I understand that she is receiving all of her rewards right now while she is in heaven.

There were not a lot of moments of reflections from my mother about her childhood. I knew that she had three sisters. However, I only had a relationship with two of my maternal aunts and her only brother. My Aunt Mamie was the eldest sibling and she lived in a nearby town.

My aunt was hard to miss at approximately six feet five inches tall and she had a personality that was larger than life. She put one in the mind of Madea because she was bold and very outspoken.

My Aunt Leatrice is the second eldest and she lived one street away from us. Aunt Lea and my mother were very different and I thought that it was strange that they were even related. They resembled each other but my aunt had a lighter skin complexion than my mom.

They got along very well but they did not visit each other much. My Aunt attended a Baptist church and she was a chain smoker and spoke her mind. My mother was quiet and attended a Pentecostal Church and abstained from alcohol, smoking and observed the Levitical law regarding her diet.

The other two siblings were also very different from my mom and a lot like my Aunt Leatrice as well. I only met my Aunt Thelma and my Uncle Otis on one occasion and they both made lasting impressions on me.

My Uncle had a hole in his throat from a stoma that he acquired from an emergency tracheostomy. He was a survivor of throat cancer and he had recovered to the point that he was able to phonate by placing a finger over the opening in his throat.

My Aunt Thelma was introduced to us under very unpleasant circumstances. My mother was summoned to their cousins house for what we thought was a family reunion. We were elated to finally meet her half sister but after we made her encounter the reunion turned dark.

My immediate family was my mom's life, but she put the LORD first in everything that she did. This was the source of conflict that her sister wanted to address with her in front of a room full of family members. Thelma had a scowl on her face and began to confront my mother about thinking that she was closer to God than she was.

Thelma began to swear while she puffed on her menthol cigarette and blew smoke into my mother's face. My sister and I were in grade school at the time and we were surprised at how her sibling was treating her.

My mother solemnly sat there and did not say one word. One could cut the tension in the room with a knife if they could find it amongst the cloud of cigarette smoke. Thelma seemed to rant on forever about how my mother grew up with nothing.

Now that Betty has a spouse, family and a big house she thinks "to hell with her other family". Thelma concluded with "nobody in this explicative room is closer to God than me and Betty you are dead to me". My mother finally responded with "so be it". My sister and I had both stood up and positioned ourselves during the disrespectful rant on each side of my mother.

We placed our hands on her shoulders and gently rubbed her back to show her love and support. That was the last time that I saw those family members again. The truth about my mother's upbringing was not reflective of Thelma's perspective at all. My mother was the youngest daughter amongst her four siblings.

Otis was the youngest and the only male child. My Aunt's allegedly had different fathers and my maternal grandmother suffered from some form of mental illness.

My Aunt Leatrice shared with me that their mother was often institutionalized because she would become detached from reality. My grandmother died while she was inpatient at a mental facility and the family had always believed that she was euthanized. My aunt stated that they gave my grandmother Bobbi the "black bottle" which was believed to be a poison to end her life.

My mother was a toddler when her mother died so she had no recollection of her. Only on rare occasions would my mother make a remark about her childhood memories. During one summer vacation I met my great Aunt Ciet and my Uncle Willie. These two proudly told me that they had raised my mother as their own child from a very young age. I was surprised to hear this because I had met my late maternal grandfather, Curtis Willis.

I asked my mother about her childhood and she stated that her father loved his women more than he loved his children so he allowed them to be given away. My mother added that she and Leatrice were supposed to be raised together with some family members.

Once the designated day arrived that they were supposed to be picked up and taken to their new home my mother was abandoned. The family members commented that they only wanted my Aunt Leatrice because she had a fair skin complexion.

Then they remarked with "Betty Lou was too black so they refused to take her home with them." I empathize with my mother because I have experienced colorism from family members and within our ethnic community.

Recently, I spoke with my Aunt Leatrice's grandson and he told me about my Aunt's first spouse. I was surprised to hear that she had been married twice. My aunt told him that the marriage had been arranged by family members and that she had fled for her life because of the abuse.

Her oppressor practiced bigamy so she was able to move on without a legal battle. My mother was not trafficked by these so called good samaritans that promised to take care of my aunt. The hue of her skin had served as a protective shield from evil.

The LORD in HIS infinite wisdom kept her chaste just like Sarah, Abraham's wife in the Bible. This woman of God's womb was deemed to be sacred in the eyes of the LORD. Betty Lou would only know her spouse and she was favored to give birth to ministers that would serve as purveyors of truth for the LORD.

My mother told me that she grew up going to a Southern Baptist Church but she did not really know the LORD. She smiled as she told me about her fondest childhood memories of laying in an open field and looking up at the big blue sky. It was there that she would talk to her real daddy, her Heavenly Father, God.

She spent countless hours pretending that she was the apple of her papa's eye. One day she said that she saw a bunch of shepherds gently guiding their sheep with the shepherd's crooks in their hands walking across the sky.

Smiling, she stated that she wished that she was an artist so she could paint the images and recreate the colors for others to see! She further explained that they had on robes with the most beautiful colors that she had ever seen. My mother stated that she desired to have the real love of a mother and a father. One day she would have a family of her own to love and they would love her too.

When my mother was fourteen years old she returned home to live with her father. One day she met a fella that was twenty one years old and he began to show an interest in her. Initially, she was not interested in him and she was known as a petite young lady that could hold her own.

She was approximately five feet five inches tall and weighed about one hundred and ten pounds. During a baseball game she was approached by the neighborhood bully Jimmy and he threatened to assault her. Betty Lou picked up a two by four and struck him in the stomach and he fell to the ground.

While Jimmy lay there motionless on the ground, the neighborhood children gathered around them to witness the conflict. Jimmy did not get up and one child yelled out "Betty we think that you killed him!"

After several minutes he regained consciousness and he stood up, caught his breath and gathered his composure. There would be no sequel to the fight. Jimmy apologized to my mother and then they became inseparable and she described him as her best friend.

Meanwhile, this twenty one year old guy continued to pursue my mother and she became attracted to him. They would visit on the front porch for two years and talk for hours throughout the week. My grandfather Curtis would turn on the light switch at dusk and it was a signal for her gentleman suitor to leave.

Betty's suitor respected her and her father. This was evident because he observed and followed the household rules. One day he asked her father for permission to take her on a date to the movie theater. My grandfather agreed and she said that when they arrived he looked into her eyes and told her that she had the most beautiful eyes in the world.

Then he told her that he had fallen in love with her and that he wanted to ask her father permission to marry her. My mother smiled in disbelief and told him that she loved him too. Her beau approached her father and asked him for his daughter's hand in marriage.

Grandfather Curtis told him 'yes' and he instructed him to take care of his "baby girl". They married and they started their new life together as Mr. and Mrs. Earlon Bell.

My mother credited my late father with properly raising her and teaching her how to become a responsible adult. He loved her and protected her as a spouse, respected her like a brother, taught her as father and nurtured her like a mother.

They were married for fifteen years before she gave birth to her first child. I remember their testimony at church of how she was barren and how they struggled with infertility.

Miraculously, she gave birth to six children, three boys and then three girls. There were never any specific details given about their battle with child bearing so I did not think about whether or not their plight was traumatic.

One day I was looking through my birth records and I read the words gravida 8 and para 6. My training as a nurse told me that my mother had at least eight documented pregnancies with six live births. I froze at that moment because I never knew that she had suffered from two miscarriages. These were the ones that she sought medical attention for and tried to salvage.

My mind began to wonder if she had experienced numerous failed attempts at conception and dealt with spontaneous abortions at home. Now their testimony of having "no hope" to have their own children one day meant even more to me.

I considered my parents overprotective and now I understood why they held onto each of their children so tightly. We were all told that we were gifts from the LORD and they had given us back to God at birth. The earliest childhood message that I remember is that I belonged to God and that I was set apart for HIS plans and purposes only. My desire is to complete the assignment that my late mother started in her earthly ministry.

I am honored to pick up the mantle that she wore in order to do the will of HIM that sent me into this earthly realm. I want to live my life, serve our LORD and die like this Magnanimous Spiritual Giant.

My mother always told us to listen to her instruction and follow her example because one day she would be "dead and gone". She would follow that up with "I do not want to lose my sight or my mind...I want the LORD to have mercy on me and take me home quickly".

My mother was lugging a refrigerator out of the back door to defrost it. Then the next week she was admitted to the hospital, diagnosed with primary gallbladder cancer with metastasis and given only six months to live.

My mother told us what she wanted to be buried in, requested to have a wake but no funeral and forbid us to allow anyone to try to resuscitate her lifeless body after death. My mother said "when I am absent from my body then I will be present with the LORD".

We took her home and two weeks later we stood around her bed and sang to her as she transitioned. *Holding my Savior's hand, viewing the promised land, nothing on earth can stop me from holding my Savior's hand.*

"Behold, he cometh with clouds; and every eye shall see him, and they *also* which pierced him: and all kindreds of the earth shall wail because of him. Even so, Amen (Revelation 1:7 KJV)."

This my dear friends is the beginning of the end.

This is Volume 1 of the Book of Betty Lou.

Volume 6

The Book of Earlon

The conclusion of the Book of Betty Lou

Genesis 17:1-2

My father was a strong and wee little man. A gentle giant and an inspiration to all that knew him. His height was around five feet six inches tall; in my personal opinion he walked as if he was ten feet tall. Earlon projected great strength and was an excellent depiction of a man with mustard seed faith. I am a self proclaimed Daddy's girl!

Most of the time he was quiet but when you spoke to him about something that he loved he could go on for hours. We had to pay close attention when our parents spoke about their childhoods if we wanted to know more.

Both of them were tight lipped with regard to specifics and they refused to give many details. One time my father ordered a birth certificate and the health department wrote him about missing information. My mother was discussing the facts with him when I overheard him tell her that he did not like his birth name.

Confused, my mother asked him what it had to do with him obtaining a birth certificate? My dad timidly looked at my mother and stated that his grandmother was partially Native American. He followed this up with "she wanted the honor of naming him as her first grandson. She chose a tribal name in order to honor her culture and he did not like her choice".

My father simply changed his name when he went to school and that was the end of her legacy. I started calling him the boy that named himself. They cleared up the confusion with the state and he was issued a birth certificate with his self proclaimed name of Earlon.

My late father was the eldest child of five children, he had three brothers and two sisters. All of his siblings respected him and they had a healthy relationship. My father rarely spoke about his childhood but he did tell us that he came from a troubled home.

My grandmother Drusillow was a Christian and he told us that she loved his father and their children. Grandpa Evage was a functional alcoholic that would abuse my grandmother, his children and he failed to provide for his family.

He was also a philanderer that would sleep with other men's wives. My father told me that his dad would go to the store to buy bread and milk for the family. Instead he would return home with liquor.

My dad would wear his shoes until the soles wore out. He learned how to cut the toes out of his shoes when he outgrew them so he would still have some shoes to wear.

One day he heard that his father had been murdered coming home from his girlfriend's house. The abuse was over but now he had to drop out of school and go to work as a child to help support his family. There were no child labor laws to restrict him from working full time so he kept two jobs.

During the day he was a cook and worked in a bakery. Then at night he worked in a movie theater that did not provide service to *coloreds*. The day job provided him with delicacies to fill his empty little belly. Whereas the night gig allowed him to have a place to sleep.

There was not a lot of time to go to church but he did have some experience with religion. Occasionally he would attend a Southern Baptist Church and engage in a church service. When he became an adult he worked as a field hand, industry worker and any odd job that would provide him with income.

As previously mentioned, he met my mother when he was twenty one years old. My dad told us that he thought that my mother had the most beautiful eyes that he had ever seen.

When he met her he knew that she was the woman that he wanted to marry. He developed a strategy to be patient with her, become her friend and respectfully ask her father if he could date her.

Once he realized that their feelings were mutual he asked her father for her hand in marriage. My dad said that he pledged to be a better spouse and father than his late dad was. He wanted to make sure that his wife and family always knew that he loved them and he wanted to support his family.

The main goal that my father had for his marriage was that they would remain married until death or Christ's return. He pledged that he would work tirelessly to provide for his wife and six children. They agreed that she would assume the role of domestic homemaker and attend to their children and home.

Their dreams seemed to be shattered when they struggled with infertility for 15 years. My father stated that he was invited to church one night by someone because he had been discouraged. There was a female evangelist preaching that night named Sister Street.

My dad told me that he was clean and well groomed that night and he was wearing a white suit. He had never heard a woman preach the gospel but he was not opposed to the idea. This woman was full of the Spirit of God and when she approached my father she prayed for him.

My dad said that he began to sob and the tears were flowing like a water faucet. Then before he knew it she said "roll" and he fell to the floor and began to dust the floor as he rolled under the benches throughout the sanctuary. He had never experienced the power of God before.

After the service he realized that he had a calling from God in his life. He joined the church and learned how to engage in the ministry of evangelism. When he returned to one of his jobs he decided to fast and pray during his lunch break instead of hang out.

His co-workers angrily approached him during their lunch break because his car was where they would smoke and drink. He told them that he was a born again believer and that his car would be locked up from now on.

Eventually, my father would become an ordained Elder in the Church of God In Christ and serve on the ministry team. During his journey of spiritual growth he was alone because my mother had remained unsaved.

He said that he invited her to church and it only made her mad. There were times that she would test him by burning his food on purpose in order to make him mad and to see if he had really changed. My father would not say a word and he would eat the burnt food and pray about it.

One day he invited my mother to church and she agreed to come but she decided to embarrass him. She wore the darkest red lipstick that she owned and placed huge clip on earrings in her ears and boldly walked into the sanctified church.

My mother told me that during the service the Spirit of God moved upon her and she was convicted by the LORD. She began to weep and repent of her sins and the earrings spontaneously fell off of her ears and secured themselves together.

She took this as a sign that the LORD wanted her to don in modest apparel in order to honor him. They had now become a power couple in the LORD and she too would operate under the mighty power of God.

They moved to Iowa and bought a home together and decided to pursue their dream of evangelism. They served in the local church as licensed ministers and became a surrogate mother and father to other people's children. As my father grew in his faith in God he was excited to share his testimony with other people in the church.

One day he had a dream about three fish that were lying next to each other. He stated that the two larger fish were closer together than the smallest fish. Through the gift of the Holy Spirit he interpreted this to mean that my mother would give birth to three son's and the elder two would be larger in size and closer in age than the youngest one.

The people in the church laughed and thought that his dream and interpretation were a false prophecy. My parents had been without children for over 15 years and they were both middle aged. My mother became pregnant with my eldest brother and within two years she would give birth to another son. My third eldest brother was more than two years younger than his two older siblings and he is much smaller in stature than both of them.

Several years would pass by and my father would have another supernatural experience and predict the birth of me and two of my sisters. The house that my parents lived in had unreliable electricity and the power source would fail. My dad had to teach my mother how to reset the braker in the basement because it happened a lot.

One day they were both resting at home and the braker needed to be switched back on. My mother was in another part of the house so she called out for my father to complete the task.

Grudgingly, he traipsed down the dark staircase with a flashlight to the braker box. Once he replenished the light source he ascended up the stairwell and there were three young girls surrounding him.
They were dressed in pink gowns and blue housecoats. One of them boldly said to him "daddy you are not going to leave us down here in the dark".

Once they reached the top of the staircase with their protector they vanished. This time he boldly gave his testimony at church and he simply sat back and waited for the promise to be fulfilled.

My eldest sister was born a few years later, then my middle sister arrived and I was born only fifteen months after her. My mother was elated to have a collection of six children even though the rapid succession of pregnancies took a toll on her health. She recalls having to crawl to take care of me and my sisters because her health was so depleted.

The LORD restored her to perfect health and she and my father were able to provide total care for us. We attended weekly church service, had in-home Bible study and did recreational activities as a family.

My parents supported us in our education and encouraged us to engage in extracurricular activities. My siblings and I are all equipped in the ministry and we use our gifts and talents to serve the LORD.

The ministry that my parents founded was in Atwood, Tennessee and they named it *Deliverance Church of God in Christ (C.O.G.I.C)*. They referred to the church as a mission because they believed that Christians should always be on the move as followers of Christ.

Their platform was geared towards winning souls for the Kingdom of God. Many people that attended and joined our church experienced the supernatural power of God and were set free from the bondage of sin.

I witnessed people get set free from drug addiction, mental health problems, illness and generational curses. Everyone that joined our church was saved, spirit filled and capable of conducting a church service.

Initially, I was resentful as a seventeen year old with the relocation. I had to leave my comfortable lifestyle in the Midwest to accompany my parents. As a teen I failed to understand why I was the only child that had to sacrifice my future plans in order to pioneer their ministry.

Since I have surrendered to God I realize that He was training me to build a ministry from the grassroots. I was prophesied to as a teen and told that I wore an Apostolic mantle. This mantle on my life was utilized to build Deliverance C.O.G.I.C. along with my parents.

We had a prison ministry and frequented the nearby government housing units in order to lead people to the LORD. We offered charity to those that were hungry and destitute and made sure that they had a ride to work and church services. We assisted in the development of other churches and gave financial contributions to support the body of Christ.

Our choir and dramatic interpretation dance team traveled to other churches and ministered to the masses. We witnessed the power of God touch the lives of all those that we encountered as we worship God through our designated ministries.

My parents had succeeded in completing their assignments unto the LORD. They were both rewarded with several arrows that manifested as descendents within their quiver. The scripture that I was inspired by the LORD for the Book of Earlon and Betty Bell comes from Genesis Chapter one, verse seventeen.

The LORD was speaking to Abraham when he was almost one hundred years old. The two were in a spiritual covenant so the LORD admonished him to cut away his flesh. This meant that the LORD wanted him to decrease as a human being and increase in his inner spiritual man.

The LORD referred to himself in this verse as *The God Almighty, El Shaddai or The Multi Breasted One*. My father mirrored his Heavenly Father when he took on several roles throughout his life and met the needs of those that were assigned to him. My father was found worthy by God to have his seed multiplied.

My dad was more than my mother's companion: he mothered, fathered, sistered, brothered and ultimately pastored her. Truly they were the answer to each other's prayers. The LORD enlarged their territory and greatly multiplied his seed.

This concludes the Book of a man with great faith, my father Pastor Earlon Bell and my miraculously, powerful mother, the amazing Betty Lou Bell. They were found worthy by El-Gibhor to produce ministers from their righteous seeds (Isaiah 9:6).

This is the Book of Earlon and concludes the volume of the Book of Betty Lou.

Volume 7
The Book of Little Robert a.k.a. Rabbitt w/ 2 t's
Isaiah 11:6

The birth announcement of my first nephew came as a bit of a shock to me for several reasons. I was a preteen and our Christian upbringing implored us to remain chaste and abstain from physical intimacy until marriage. Nonetheless, there was an increase in the number of teenage parents and our family was no exception to this growing trend.

My brother had been dating a young lady and the two teens had become inseparable. Regardless of how anyone felt about the situation, a baby was on the way. I was not going to be the baby of the Bell family anymore, I was going to be an aunt. My nephew was born and he resembled his father, Robert Senior and he brought new life into our home. My mother would keep him for weeks at a time to allow his mother to rest.

My mother loved to give people nicknames and she lovingly named him her Little Rabbitt. The events surrounding his conception, birth announcement and some of his parents' life decisions were made very rapidly. The nickname Rabbitt seemed fitting to me. I spent a lot of time with my nephew because I had the most free time as a preteen. My other siblings were in the workforce or focused on their future education goals.

My nephew was very close to my parents and he spent countless hours in our home. Over time I felt like he was my younger sibling and I invested a lot of time taking care of him. Robert was a happy toddler and he was loved and adored by his maternal and paternal families.

Although his parents did not remain together they put their personal feelings aside and allowed him to continue his routine of living between two residences. As Robert began to grow up he took on the attributes of my parents. He would spend reading his Bible, watch religious films and participate in church activities.

My sister began calling him preacher which is a nickname that my mother gave to my late father. Over time Little Robert's father moved on and fell in love with another woman and they got married. This created some tension between his parents because my brother had fathered two daughters with two different women.

I remember my nieces approaching me when they were school age and asking me if they were twins. I thought that the question was odd until they told me that their ages were the same. They wanted me to explain to them how they had different mothers and were the same age. Once I realized what they were asking me I simply replied with "go and ask your father."

There became a remarkable difference in Robert during his prepubescent years and he seemed to long for a deeper connection with his father. Shortly after he began attending grade school my family moved to another state. My interactions with him were limited to summer vacations and random visits.

The Rabbitt that I was familiar with seemed lost and was struggling with his identity. Around this time he began to get into trouble at school for unethical conduct. There were numerous times that he would run away from my parents home and I was recruited to track him down. It was apparent that he was struggling with where he belonged in life because he had lost the stability that he had in our home.

My parents offered for him and his sister to come and live with us for a while. Their mother agreed to allow them to relocate and they moved down south. The two of them enrolled in school and reintegrated into their previous family routine with us.

Their father lived across town with his wife and their two siblings and occasionally they would go and visit them. One day my nephew asked his father why they could not live with him. His father replied by telling him that there was limited space in his three bedroom home for seven people.

Rabbitt and his sister would remain at their grandparents house but continue to have access to their father. Rabbitt accepted the response with great sadness but he felt like it was better than not having a relationship with his father at all.

The older Robert became it seemed like his life became more of a roller coaster ride with periods of serenity mixed with reckless behaviors. It was unclear if there was a rush of hormones and adrenaline affecting him or if he was experiencing emotional pain. One year my parents had a discussion with Robert senior about adopting his two children.

The children had not seen their mother in several months and she had other children to take care of. They reasoned that his older two children needed consistency, structure and a routine that involved a household with two stable parents.

They retained an attorney to start the process of legal adoption and they were met with an unexpected resistance from the children's mother. I understand as a mother that it would be painful to lose custody of my children. I also witnessed the struggles within this blended family so I sympathized with my niece and nephew as well.

The court proceedings took place and the children were ordered to return home with their mother. There were mixed feelings about the final decision but all parties respected the judge's decision.

My nephew was a preteen and he was at a point in his life that he wanted more independence, he voiced to us that he had "won" a victory that day in court. Initially when his younger sister heard his declaration she was overcome with happiness but when she learned that they had to relocate without us she burst into tears.

My nephew would call me and we would catch up on how our lives were faring. There was an artificial crudeness in his words that created great concern within me. Whenever I would attempt to dive deep within his psyche he would block my attempts and reassure me that "everything is fine". Spiritually I discerned that he was running away from his feelings and that he was on a slippery slope.

I would pray for him and try to encourage him in the LORD to hold on to all of the teachings that he had received while living with us. My nephew would lighten up and I would feel a glimmer of hope that he would remember the LORD and remain faithful.

One day I received a phone call from my late Aunt Clementine and she urged me to contact my nephew so he would surrender to law enforcement. She went on to explain that he was named as a person of interest in a serious criminal matter. The rumor was that he was "wanted dead or alive". I began to pray for him and I was unable to locate him on the phone.

The LORD answers prayers because he turned himself in to the police and cooperated with the investigation. My nephew was convicted of a felony and served time in federal prison. While he was incarcerated he contacted me and I lovingly admonished him to return to the LORD.

He repented of his sins and bonded with the inmates that identified as believers and served God while incarcerated. Once he was released he continued in his walk to serve the LORD and he started a family. I was happy for him and I was grateful that he was on the right path.

Oftentimes, he would reach out to me and tell me about his accomplishments, struggles and about everyday life in general. He became the father of two beautiful children and expressed a strong desire to have a relationship with them.

At one time he was seeking acceptance so he developed an affiliation with a gang and pledged loyalty to their cause. Now he was serving the LORD so he renounced that commitment and exclusively pledged his allegiance to God.

Many years passed by, my mother died and this brought my family together for her burial. My nephew came with his children and we reunited and shared niceties and pledged to remain connected. He told me that he suffered in silence for many years after he returned home from court. His life was not what he had expected it to be so he blamed his mother for his misery.

Once he learned that my mother had died he felt like she died of a broken heart because she had lost her Little Rabbitt. I told him that was endearing but that she had health problems that were unrelated to grief or sadness. My mother had accepted the will of God that came down as the judgment from the court. My parents were both in their sixth and seventh decade of life and raising two teenagers would have been unfair to all four of them.

My nephew seemed comforted with those words and he stated that he had been working on forgiving both of his parents for feeling abandoned by them. I told him that I would pray for him and that I was proud of his spiritual maturity.

Once they departed from the south I received a phone call from the department of corrections and my nephew was institutionalized again. He humbly explained that he had messed up but he planned to get back on track again.

I sent him a book that I felt would help him on his spiritual journey about discipline. We regularly spoke on the phone and I would make sure that he was remaining steadfast in the LORD. After serving time he returned to society and told me that he was done with the criminal justice system.

Rabbitt took a special interest in cooking and he began catering to make money for his family. This young man found purpose and solace in food service to others. Robert found joy in sharing his love of cooking and this was how he would show others his love.

Many years passed and he seemed to be staying on track but I had difficulty keeping up with him. I would call his cell phone and the number would either be disconnected or the carrier had changed ownership. I worried about him but I remained faithful and kept lifting my baby up in prayer.

Out of nowhere I received a phone call from him and he was striving to remain faithful to the LORD but he found himself wrestling against many demons including substance abuse and sexual sin. He openly discussed his temptation from seducing spirits and stated that he had developed anxiety so he was treating his symptoms with alcohol.

I prayed with him and discussed strategies to combat the forces of darkness in his life. Then I spoke a prophetic word over his life and warned him to avoid the temptation to engage in criminal activity because I feared that he would end up institutionalized again.

Robert was dating a young lady and she was pregnant with his third child. He stated that they had been struggling financially and in the past he could hussle and obtain thousands of dollars within a short period of time. Alarmed I warned him that the path to destruction is broad and the way to salvation and righteousness is narrow.

I instructed him to stay on the path that is least traveled. A few days later my nephew called me and I could barely understand his words through his tears and appreciation for support.

Robert had received three contracts to cook for local pubs and his girlfriend was blessed with two job opportunities that would provide for them. I praised the LORD with him for breakthrough and reminded him that we are God, our Heavenly Father's responsibility.

A few days later I received a phone call that my nephew was in trouble with the law and that he was incarcerated. I was saddened and upset that he had let the enemy deceive him into relinquishing his spiritual inheritance from the LORD.

I took a season of silence and solitude because I did not want to discourage him by speaking out of my emotions. The LORD revealed to me that the fear of responsibility and of failure had drawn him back into old familiar habits. Nonetheless, I know that Jesus is a habit breaker and that I would continue to fight on behalf of this man of God.

Little Robert is called for such a time as this, the age of peril. The world will see the greatness of God through the deliverance that will come to his life. I asked the LORD for strategy in order to see my nephew set free for once and for all.

Finally, I received a call from my nephew and he was all fired up and began to read me scriptures. I silenced him and told him that it was time for him to get free from this spiritual bondage once and for all. He challenged me and I began to speak under the influence of the Holy Spirit and took authority over the generational curses of sin in his life.

I called out the spirit that was tormenting him over his childhood traumas and spoke of the freedom and liberty that only God can bring. Initially, he denied that he had suffered from any form of trauma. Then I told him that we only have a few minutes on the phone so I needed him to listen.

I challenged him to be brave enough to repent and ask God to search him for everything that is in him that is not like God and to really cast all of his cares on God.

The call ended and a few days later my nephew called me back from the prison. He told me that anger had risen up within him against me and that he had to decide if he wanted to hang up on me or listen.

Obviously, he listened, then he further explained that his nickname was *Sneak* and that he was capable of great deception. He described himself as a master manipulator and said that I was not fooled by his facade.

Then he told me that I had spoken to his inner man so strongly that it reminded him of his Granny Bell. My nephew broke down and cried and shared with me things that he had never told anyone. I have his permission to share that when he returned to his former home after the judge's decision he was sexually assaulted.

This led him into a deep depression and to feelings of vulnerability that made him decide to join a gang. He sought protection from harm and he wanted to appear to be tough like the members within his gang. The trauma caused him to spiral out of control and it led to him engage in reckless sexual sins and substance abuse.

Although he heard the voice of God throughout his life he was angry that the LORD allowed him to experience so much heartache and pain. How could he connect with a Heavenly Father that his grandfather and biological father preached about when he had no consistent representation of a father here on earth? I told him under the influence of the Holy Spirit that the LORD was going to totally deliver him from this bondage and use him mightily.

Robert is a prophetic watchman and he is going through his spiritual bootcamp while imprisoned. I am assigned to speak to the hurt little boy within him first and then we can concentrate on building up the grown man.

Once he is spiritually liberated and released from his prison then all will witness the power of God through this young man. After you have gone through the fire my dear sweet Rabbitt then you WILL come forth as pure gold.

The word that I want to impart into my nephew comes from Isaiah Chapter eleven verse six. "Leopards will lie down with young goats, and wolves will rest with lambs. Calves and lions will eat together and be cared for by little children" (Isaiah 11:6)".

You Little Rabbitt are the child that is chosen to fulfill this prophecy. The power of God that rests upon your life will quiet the terror that is brought on by the fear of wild animals such as the leopards, wolves and lions.

The anointing of God from your struggles will cause the things that appear fierce to others to submit and lie down like sheep and goats under the soft spoken sound of your voice.

You will exercise the dunamis power of God and the forces of darkness will retreat at the recognition of Jesus Christ that lives within you. The lifestyle that you have lived is your training ground. Surely, you discern the schemes and tactics of the enemy and defeat HIM.

You are winning, and you will continue to win whether you are on the mountain top or in the valley. The LORD promises to never leave you or forsake you (Heb 13:5). God wastes nothing, so He is using every life experience to advance your faith within HIS Kingdom.

This is why the LORD has saved the best for last. You my dear sweet son are the conclusion of *Spiritual Oatmeal and Holy Grits for the Soul.*

About the Author
Prophetess Bobby known as
Brightfame a.k.a Bobby w/ a 'y'.

Bobby is a born again spirit filled believer that loves to do the work of the LORD. She is a single parent of two adult children that work alongside her in the *Wolfpack Ministry of Deliverance*. They reside in the state of Tennessee and work in the Healthcare Industry.

Bobby writes under the pseudonym of Brightfame because her name literally translates into those two words, *Bright* and *fame*. She has written for the local paper and appeared on the local news stations to minister about health and wellness. In her spare time she advocates for the underprivileged and she is an activist for those in need.

The lifelong training that she received from her late parents Earlon and Betty Bell equipped her for the five fold ministry. The strategy that her parents developed was to use their home and church life to ensure that she would walk out her earthly ministry under the power and direction of the Holy Spirit.

Bobby recounts her earliest childhood memories in her autobiography, *Beauty from Ashes: accept that you are beautifully human and perfectly flawed.* Then she tells about how she wrestled with God in order to be accepted into secular culture. Ultimately, she shares how the pain of rejection and betrayal while living in rebellion against God led her to surrender to the LORD.

Spiritual oatmeal and Holy Grits for the soul is a cathartic dose of reality that shares real life testimonies of believers. We are the sixty-seventh book of the Bible and it is important for us to share our struggles, faith and victories with other people in order to encourage them through written Epistles.

The Bible says that "they overcame *him* (meaning the evil one), by the blood of the lamb and the word of their testimony (Revelation 12:11).

The Wolfpack Ministry is birthed to reconcile the unbeliever back to Christ and to bring deliverance to those that are captive. My prayer is for this devotional to aid you in the transformation of your mind, body and soul.

As always I most sincerely remain,
Brightfame a.k.a. Bobby w/ a 'y'.

Jen

Rebecca and her child

Pastor Earlon Bell

First Lady Betty Lou Bell

Pastor Emmanuel & First Lady Eunice

Rabbitt with two t's

I would like to give a special thanks to my Wolfpack cubs for their support and dedication of this project. My daughter, The Indestructible One and my son, Israel Bell. They spent their Saturday afternoon helping me design the book cover.

Thank you for the faithful service that you give to GOD and for your contributions to the ministry! I Love Youse Twose to the moon and back, around the world and back again!

Love, Mommycakes

Made in the USA
Columbia, SC
26 August 2024

41204647R00074